ALSO BY RICHARD KENNEY

The One-Strand River
The Invention of the Zero
Orrery
The Evolution of the Flightless Bird

TERMINATOR

TERMINATOR

POEMS, 2008–2018

Richard Kenney

ALFRED A. KNOPF

NEW YORK

2019

THIS IS A BORZOI BOOK
PUBLISHED BY ALFRED A. KNOPF

Copyright © 2019 by Richard Kenney

All rights reserved. Published in the United States by Alfred A. Knopf, a division of Penguin Random House LLC, New York, and in Canada by Penguin Random House Canada Limited, Toronto.

www.aaknopf.com

LIBRARY OF CONGRESS CATALOGING-IN-PUBLICATION DATA
Names: Kenney, Richard, author.
Title: Terminator : poems, 2008–2018 / Richard Kenney.
Description: First edition. | New York : Knopf, 2019.
Identifiers: LCCN 2019002031 (print) | LCCN 2019003045 (ebook) |
    ISBN 9780525656647 (ebook) | ISBN 9780525656630 (hardback)
Subjects: BISAC: POETRY / American / General.
Classification: LCC PS3561.E443 (ebook) | LCC PS3561.E443 A6 2019
    (print) | DDC 811/.54—dc23
LC record available at https://lccn.loc.gov/2019002031

Jacket art and design by Tyler Comrie

Manufactured in the United States of America
First Edition

For Carol and Maeve, Hollis and Will

CONTENTS

III. *World Enough*

IV. *Personae*

VII. *Portrait of a Gentleman*

VIII. *Personae*

XI. *Vanishing*

TERMINATOR

Definitions

Word: an interval,
a needle biopsy
of a waterfall,

making digital
the rinse of experience
by jot and tittle.

Poetry, I think,
is the distant-thunder sound
in the drying ink.

Annunciation

Imagine a loved face reflecting on the side-
edge of a scimitar-shaped shard

of a breaking mirror—just thus
it was: sun-whet suddened at the oculus

of the Pantheon one day,
just barely, along its under

eyelid—
Look! Eyeliner, I said,

unimaginatively,
and you looked. That genitive

moment was too long, by an age.
You saw the sickle, not its just-touched edge,

that thinnest paring of light released,
lasting

less long
than a whetstone's ring.

Because then the image began to oxidize
and thicken, smear, fade, as bronze does,

as everything eyestruck does, once
announced

into a noun.

Terminator

The Terminator
is the line separating—
not the hemispheres,

that's the Equator—
but the one separating
certain metaphors.

One terminator:
that knapped core, the inner curve
of the crescent moon.

Another, later
in our romance, that scythe-swerve
down the face of soon.

One is the future
severing, leaving the past
to its own story.

One a new suture
down the calvarium of
memento mori.

I.

ANYWHERE

NOT PARIS

Our shimmer of days

sucked through the howling wall-clock's

macerating blades—

Signs

Slung
like an ancient
baseball

across
long
space

past Ursa
Major
enter

invisible
the Cybele
Meteor

unwelcome
in the Milky
Way

or so
we'll
wager

*

Look up, Alley Oop!—
pressure-flaking a flint core
in your unflown coop,

Deep Time, that egg-blown
old dark under the Dordogne—
there's blood on your door:

Somethings in the sky—
something's scratched your cornea—
blink. Don't rub your eye.

*

Tell, Sibyl, huffing sulfur,
intuiting tomorrow,
your mind's reticulum in shreds,
your vital signs a horror:

They've seized the Cybele Meteor.
They're bringing it to Rome.
Is that a good idea?
Gaia grim in a black stone?

Anywhere Not Paris

1. Edges

About the time one starts to grow suspicious
of the world, to lose one's faith in edges,
verges, borders, boundaries, that cusp
comes at which one's own biology
begins to cross them with abandon. Bulge
and salient balancing retreat: here hair-
line and shrunk shank, there the more general her-
niations supervene: belly occludes belt;
dewlaps brim the buttoned collar.

*

Deeper pattern shatters. Ventricular
percussions stutteringly muff the rhythm
of a lifetime: *lub-dub-dub*: the world's withering
fire. Grotesque foreign proteins trickle
though the blood-brain barrier. *Not-You*
enters the city in triumph, to clarions and cheers,
while *You* hammer the portcullis, howling. Does Nature
have edges? Tell me that, you smudge, you faint Venn
diagram whose membrane-lines have proven solvent
in the stream of things?

*

As words as vessels
fail to hold their little maelstroms, all selves
lose outline, so. Nouns leak; verbs leak worse,
and that's the news. Our poor suppressor cells

don't recognize us any more than What's-Her-
Name, from whenever-it-was, fumbling words
with me on the street the other day. She, too,
shape-shifted like a blink of myth: Ishtar
Resartus in a paisley shawl; Apollo reappareled
in papyrus and bone—what a pair!
Say, Siri—Pythia—what's flesh anyway but shadow-
garb a gone god's doffed? If ours seemed a touch
déclassé, it's only by unfair comparison
with what divinity was wearing in—I want to say *Paris,
1972?*—Good grief, she was a pretty
Muse!—

        And who's not shapelier today than soon,
a thousand years or so from now, redistributed
according to surfactant properties
of Time? Her name?— I want to say Beauty,
though it might have been Betty. The point is, even proper
nouns bleed out like all the rest of us.

*

Not the street, the bus. It was on the bus.

2. *Taxa*

To my friend the physicist, who still resembles
his yearbook picture, things seem simple.

Acknowledging her name, conceding her avian
properties, her moods, her modes, her raving

beauty, he'll insist she is a *mammal*, and feel
the firmer settlement of saying something real.

I ask: are avian dinosaurs, *qua* birds,
reptiles? And then my friend and I have words.

3. Under the Oculus

Turn the mirror edgewise, time sideways,
so to speak. Here's the waist
of the hourglass, our porthole oculus,
cervix of the future
which, like everything accelerated,
swells
and thins:
thus
memory shreds in the solar wind,
the quartz porthole, bleb on a blowpipe, spills,
the skull rises through the face
behind its mica visor, slung in the centrifuge—
no refuge:
lick the mirror like a glacier,
like aluminum in winter—
lick Antarctica, that'll slow your bosons,
won't it?

4. Unlikely,

we say, involuntarily invoking a Land of Unlikeness
where no echo augurs a far shore,
nothing accrues to a human cry.
The mirror like Loch Ness

coughs up its plesiosaur.
A decade ricochets by.
Hear the Doppler foghorn through the shaving glacier?
Check its edges, calving.

Having
read somewhere that certain sorts of humor
depend upon surprise, a sly
low-slung irruption of the unexpected, I—
oh, my!
That's why the mirror gets so *funny*.

5. *Don't make me laugh,*

we say, meaning something like, *No.*
About the time we stop stropping like barbers these blades
of nouns and verbs against the spinal cord,
the hard thought having once for all occurred
they'll never prove keen enough to resect the clade
from the light-waves washing all this flotsam in—

About our lot: loss.
About the courage one might wish to summon,
about that sang-
froid, the saying-goodbye sans tears—

About the time (as I was saying)
one starts to grow suspicious of the lexicon,
to lose faith in defensible frontiers,
to sicken
somewhat before the calving berg
of the funhouse mirror (horribly

a liquid, as the pedant puts it), the glass bags
in and out, flimmering like a windy bubble:

Now here's belt uncinched, subtending belly
now debouching
into neighboring space—

Feel that elevator-lurch-and-pause?—

And now Biology
like punched dough no more plump and jowly
bugles its retreat: cheeks scoop; thews
thin. The world's fire withering.
And still a good deal left to lose.

6. So, for the moment

never mind the Time Machine, that ever-cracking mirror,
syntax, cervix of the sandglass, oculus, our kind's quartz
porthole blown like a soapy bubble flimmering through the
Kuiper Belt and Oort Cloud, occluded at the terminator,
minatory as it is in mind, always, us tongue-stuck, indistinct
in a moon-calf wince windmilling backward—what an
image!—into origins or epitaphs, it's life, still, though
thought stall,

and not the worst laugh ever laughed.

The Time Machine

1. The Pantheon

Watch, at the stoneless cope
of the open oculus, its keen kerf
slice Time. Acetylene sun—

ice moon—the strobe
accelerates. Earth's verdure
winking in the onset:

instants!—seasons!—eons!—the snow-globe
spinning like a pitched ball back the coffered curvature,
all its flakes a flurry of unsettling—

*

Now wing-whirr of the four-foot dragonfly—
Pock-ploops the early asteroidal rain-drum din—
A blood-red placental moon drapes a third of the sky—
Whoops!—now lithosphere slips like pudding-skin—
Syntax enters the ape—the world splinters—
Enter invisible: the Cybele Meteor spins past Pluto—

*

Pilot-
less, queasy, we lisp *Abort!*
The time machine creaks to a halt.
Through its quartz porthole
the page stretches, endless, white as salt.

2. When Are We?

After tree ferns, their whispery soughing;
after predator-drone-sized darning-needle's whizz.
After armored fish
dragged up clanking from the benthos.
After Amazon and Congo run confluent.
Certainly after our one moon tore off, dripping,
but well before aurochs
(great big aurochs bumping our cavewall,
oilcanning our cavewall,
denting it to get in!—
a flock of handprints pushing back—)
After also smilodon, dawn horse.
Well after that dead stegosaur
with its plates unstacked,
its veined tongue lolling,
dirt-stuck, breaded like schnitzel—
(note iridescence on the oily onyx shell
of the stag beetle staggering
up the medial valley
of the dead stegosaur's lolling tongue—

*

Zoom out:
Iridescence streaks the lens
against a thick galactic talc.
As though as hoar
from a pane
the great corrugated thumbnail of God
scrapes a starless line
across the screeching empyrean—

*

3. The Meteor

Well, that was how it was. Maybe we dreamt it.
That was a ride. Time torn open like a hydrant.
That was sure hair unbound and lips apart,
lapels aflutter in the flume of the photon-torrent.
We stood looking up, and a bit of iron scratched the oculus,
and that was just our luck,
start to finish, we fishtailed, and treed,
and fell, and it didn't kill us,
though the hands horrored up
and we hit the quartz screen,
and it starred.

Madsong

Origins suggest edges;
middles, too, as also ends;
the horsehide baseball just so sketches
an arc from hickory to fence

(whose little horse, just poodle-high,
once fled the sabertooth's embrace)
but here the ball is said "to fly"
above the runner and the base,

the flaxen laces spinning, spun
like inks in the Book of Kells;
thus Africa was somewhere once,
the Arctic somewhere else—

as also, too, magnetic north
and also, too, Polaris,
and this and that and so and forth,
recalling me to Paris:

I meant *appearances,* I think,
like a scholar in a study—
The Keats Equation!—sing, sing,
since her name must have been Beauty.

II.

SCIENCE

TUESDAY

Fragment

There's nothing any-

where but guessing. [Frag. thirty-

four, Xenophanes.]

Conceptual Thinking

> A polyp would be a conceptual thinker if a feeling of
> "Hollo! thingumbob again!" ever flitted through its mind.
> —WILLIAM JAMES

Re Names:

Finical,
perception
its pen-knife,

nerve-long
language
feels for an edge,

teasing out the rim
of a perimeter,
muttering

Hollo?— Polyp
to Apollo:
Bob's your uncle,

Mr. James

Agnostic Gospels

Do I believe in Fahrenheit degrees?
Of course I do, they're real enough, as, please
the little gods, also the little gods,
and big ones, too, but grudgingly, the odds
against them feeling somewhat longer. Muse,
too, who hardly ever calls. Also the news
from what used to be called Frontiers of Science. *Science!*
that mortgaged curator of psychic sins,
in this case Curiosity: what killed his
cat may serve his proudest faculties
the same, since Reason scums its petri dish,
endangered now, with every wilting wish.

But weren't we speaking of *belief*? Schrödinger's cat?
What's reason got to do with that?

Reason May Not Mean to Be the Sophist

Slip the Problem from its sleeve. The vinyl's
scratched. And that's the problem, finally:

the nature of emotion's analog,
while languages are digital. Too few long-

playing feelings, inkily remastered,
long survive by heart. This mystery

runs deep, requiring deeper magics. *Look,* we
say, by darksome sleight ventriloquy,

referring to a nerve potential triggered
by a pressure in the world, recurring

now in a lung, in a laugh, in a poem of Sappho's.

Schrödinger's Elephant

Once upon a time in Copenhagen
the blind men met to scratch the quantum noggin.

They hashed things out, agreeing to decree
that the wave function of the pachyderm
collapses into rope, or spear, or tree,
or fan, or wall, as senses will confirm,

but only when the moment's brought to measure.
Till then, it's all-and-none. It's worse than Escher.

The key, you'll note, is human observation.

Human?— How in heaven's name?—

                                    The answer's
mathematical as all Creation,
involving Probability and Chance. . . .

Laypeople simply can't—look, no offense,
but try now not to think of elephants.

Science Tuesday

The first human-chimpanzee chimera,
christened *Pan sapiens,* was born today
at Brigham and Women's Hospital, in Boston.

The Hubble's Very Wide Spool camera
regained partial function of its data
module, and is now on track for the Sirius starburst.

Dr. 32B, chief of research at Merck,
again replied, "No comment." "Ever," he added,
to op-ed columns suggesting he's hostile to the Press.

The Sentient Rover, assembled in America
from Chinese parts, parked since Saturday
in a no-load zone on Mars, appears depressed.

Spokesmen for the Generation Meerkat
Energy Corp. assured critics that the shudder is soldered,
stressing again that "containment vessel" is at best

a metaphor. The starburst—a miracle!
The drug had side effects. The Rover broke. The "baby satyr,"
Pan sapiens, died at his surrogate mother's breast.

He was hard to look at, she is reported to have said.

Pan sapiens *2*

The first human-chimpanzee chimera
looked searchingly into the shaving mirror.
His hairline—was it?—yes, it was advancing.
Another blow, albeit only glancing.
For, having clever fingers (who'd forced fire?)
he'd simply boost the amps in his blow dryer.

Later, glaciers shrank from their moraines.
Seas rose above the knees of fishing cranes.

Venice, once resembling Tycho's Mars
now swamped like Venus, where the brontosaurs
rent heaven with hoarse hoots in praise of gods
who lent such swanny necks to sauropods.
And if you can't believe a noon so strange,
consult your own defunct nouns, for a change.

The Blank Slate

Concerning Common Ancestors, in verse:

Might chimpanzees once raised by bonobos
reach deep into your trousers and propose
engagements polymorphous and perverse?
Who knows.

Or would (here note initial terms reversed)
a bonobo by chimpanzees once nursed
and raised to adolescence come to blows,
or worse?

The question is an old one, cast in fable—
the oldest one, maybe, rephrased by Abel,
marking Cain, the line forever cursed—
though what an ape'll

say to that (in ASL, of course,
if non-recursive, and a touch terse)
may not refer to the matter of the Apple,
or Ancestors

at all. Or Babel.

And never mind what it means to say "refers."

Pan sapiens *3*

I am *Pan sapiens.* I don't speak well,
and so I write. Some say I look like hell.
I think that's hard. I think I look like you.
Pan in, however—never mind the view:

You've seen it all your life, the diorama
stinking with the crowd of us, from *Rama-*
pithecus to poor Neanderthal,
who's lost his lisp at last, and, standing tall
peers like any fool into my eyes
where once upon a time, a wild surmise—

Now, dip your quill into the pupils' ink:
it isn't how we look. What is it? *Think.*

The Arcturan Vivisectionist Explains

This specimen's common name is *Mirroreye.*
Observe (retractor, please) just *here*—a rare
non-adaptive anomaly in the so-called third
lid—common enough, of course, in lizards, birds,
sharks, et al., all perfectly unremarkable, save
that the nictitating membrane is *silvered*
inside, enabling these creatures to see themselves
reflected *everywhere:* in wood-grain, in moon, in clouds,
in others of their kind, even; also imparting an odd,
not uncrabwise aspect to their gait, backing hell-bent,
headlong, as it were, into what's already happened.

Horcrux: A Romantic Landscape

—AS SCORED FOR CRUMHORN BY EDWARD LEAR

You need some genes for jumping,
but none for not jumping too high,
since that information is stored on location,
between the earth and sky.

Our ancestors hadn't to worry
about too many sweets before lunch.
What protected their livers? The veldt could deliver
just so many berries per bunch.

Memory is a secretion
externally fertilized, so,
that a landscape revisited still may elicit
a shiver from ancient snow.

Some writers have interesting minds;
most don't. Yet by poem or novel
they somehow find thoughts the way tubers in plots
may surface, when stirred with a shovel.

The brain thinks it does all the thinking,
but likely it doesn't, at that:
too much information is stored on location.
It couldn't be done from a vat.

As birds need genes for flying
but none for returning to ground,
and the human mind is not born blind
to the conditions of its surround,

if the world's a bouquet of answers
to the questions the senses pose,
its lies of omission would be the conditions
that Heaven only knows.

Forget what you can't imagine,
the edge of the measure of man:
since what's unfurled as the sum of the world
must be what you can.

And that's not terrible news.
It means we *are* some place.
That's some reassurance. Where it leaves the Arcturans?—
But Lunch is served. Say grace.

Brains in a Vat

Step inside, please, spake the elevator,
hissing, reminiscent of Lord Vader
also in its little shudder. Later,
lobbed, too, through the black hole labeled Vela
X-1, judging by an indicator
blinking upward through the blank abyss
between the tenth and millionth floors, the Muse
of Relativity would disabuse
me of my geocentrism, for this
was Einstein's gravitational caboose,
and I was in a thought experiment.
Or was one, which is what I might have meant.
Still, the simplest things seem paramount:

That elevator *talked,* and I can count.

Numbers

Seethe on silicon
like bacterial plaques.
Somehow they liken

to appearances.
They have a seemliness from
which all earth rinses.

Elegance! Log on:
the algorithm resets
as *LaOcOOn*.

Unlikeness yaws thought.
Timor mortis is the thought.
That land Time forgot.

This—no mere mirror.
Nor is an error message
like no tomorrow.

Ecological Meditation,

or Space Is Closer Than Chicago

Even from Peoria.
Much closer, on the flat.
The wide yonder's wide indeed;
foil-thin, for all that.

The mountains puncture most of it,
their human climbers, too,
who wriggle dressed in oxygen
to a sky scarcely blue,

where helicopter blades won't bite
and sound itself thins.
A fifty-minute walk at most
on legs which once were fins.

The sea is similar, whose deeps
a dipstick shows as shallows:
wet an apple—that's the earth,
a scarcely moistened chalice.

What to make of thoughts like these
when the mind wants a yonder
wide enough to hold itself?—
I don't know. I wonder.

Horcrux Redux,

or Good Luck

I recall the earlier lecture, now
(or the fact in verse inflected)
that the human genome turned out somehow
to be "smaller than expected."

You need genes to rise off earth,
to crawl or jump or fly—
for all baroqueries of birth,
if none to fall or die.

The operator's manual
for returning to dirt, they say,
is locked in the physics of fare-thee-well,
not in the DNA.

It's so for so much else in life,
like appetite for sugar.
There's only *Go*. To add a *Stop*
the box would have had to be bigger.

Now, thinking of the Pleistocene
while reading above the fold,
reflecting on rapacity
and limits in a world

which vomits hordes of murderous apes,
eyes afire, amok
(to summarize what history
forecasts for human luck)

I could wish a few more base pairs
had been salted down the helix
to stitch us more securely to
the future: *Homo felix*.

The Drake Equation

1. They Were a Kind of Solution

Say one Spaceman, when she lands, will touch
down in a human sentence, speaking Dutch,
a dialect of Mentalese. Her torch-

song (loosely rendered from the Arcturan): "Baby
Let's Get Square with π," or "You're the Apple
of My Eye," or "Boola Theta Babel

Bye-Bye." It might make sense. This is a heady
thought. The traditional verse, *viz.* "Who's Your Daddy,"
as sung in *The War of the Worlds,* and signaled *Mayday,*

mayday—a little like Beethoven's 4th in digital
redaction—may underpin what limbic Dutch
must once upon a time have bloomed beneath the sagittal
crest of *Homo*—

       Who? What? This news just in!—the starry
sky is empty. Spacemen are out. Sorry.

2. Exo-Statisticians Change Minds, Cite Insufficiency
of Planetary Bodies of Right Type

What, no aliens? Or, with greater dignity,
life elsewhere in the universe? That window's
shut, we learn. Astronomers, indignant

desert birds, eyes screwed to the long cinder-
scuttles of their telescopes, will voice some doubt,
one hopes! This is too *lonely.* Heliocentric

humility's a habit hard to shake. Endowed
with what we've called "intelligence," or "powerful
intelligence," like-minded creatures, each an end-

point in a home-world's evolutionary raffle,
well, just *must* across the vasty deeps of space
and time yearn forth to find each other with awful

big radios. That's how the Book of Revelations
we knew used to read, rephrased so, π be praised.

3. Binary

My friend the Geometer, when asked if π
were in the sky or in the skull, replied

π's the pontification of a ratio.
Bisected, so, the circle: π. To show

that in a well-formed sentence, well, that's human, sure.
All language is. So ever since that fateful shore

of Lake Turkana where tongue forked, where first
flaking syntax split the atom into force

and mass, thing and verb, the copula
has groped to reanneal it: *this* opulence

is equal to the sum of *those* simplicities. . . .
So here's the mystery: across the placid

surface of the water a salt of stars
once scattered, hissing. Caliban stammered *Are*

stars. Then, *Look, look up at the stars!*

4. *Prose Obtrusion Concerning the Keats Equation*

Hold it there.

Would you say, whereas Beauty is a recognition of *the world*, that Truth's an attribute of *sentences*?

So that mysterious predictive gift of mathematics is precisely that of sentences like *I predict the sun will rise tomorrow*?—isn't *that* the leap that left the chimpanzees behind?—and adding time of sunrise just adds increment to the precision?

So that Platonic realm where mathematics *must* exist to be discovered by Ramanujan or Hardy or Arcturans tucked in anywhere in Time or Space is *just* that space where earlier equations live, like *love's a rose* or *tears are rain,* which Hardy's *and* Ramanujan's respective ancestors discovered independently?

That if in England *two men feed a horse, the horse stays thin,* the axiom would hold as well for two Tibetan yaks or fat Jurassic stegosaurs (assuming less that that's what the Arcturans use to carry mail than that, like us, they pinch their pence)—

That *that's* the realm where poems and equations likewise lie unspoken, quietly awaiting their *discovery?*

And so those famous instances where mathematics efflorescing on some blackboard purely for the play of it turn out to have a shocking congruence with patterns in the world is just *exactly* like the case where poetry is news before the news it stays?

That hadn't the acclaimed predictive potency of mathematics best be cast as *a reminder of forgotten shock*—the shock our shaggy kind must once have felt, framing for the first time well-formed sentences about the world that was, and then about the world about to be, and so extended human sensibility and thrust it forth as backward through the night of Time?

Yes, if diffidently.

5. Postscriptum

The aliens are back, incidentally. Astral
systems dropping planets like nuts in May. Exo-
biology leaps again into likelihood. A straw
poll proves the numbers may be multiplex.

No small relief for this slow versifier,
who, peering through this poem's decades-long zoom-
lens has seen what changes?—sapphire
heaven bleached of all biology?—*shazam!*—

and then revivified, less abruptly,
with a thought. In the same blink of the clock
the pupil of a black hole was seen to matter,
some dinosaurs grew feathers, and (this one for Ripley's)
Pluto got demoted from a planet to a rock.
Also my family died. Also I had a daughter.

III.

WORLD

ENOUGH

That parabola?

Galileo. See also:

bola, *and* hula.

The Problem

Feeling can't defend itself
in the court of reason
where every jot's accounted for,
minus frisson.

But logic has its own failures
in the bed of love,
(of which there's sometimes these days too much
speaking of).

The court of reason?—what is that
but a closed fist uncurled?
The bed of love?—what is that,
but the world?

How?

As hours back up in the clogged drain
of the glassy water clock,

as the assignation of the wind and spun vane—
I'll love you as the foghorn vague in rain—

Magnetic swipe to the blinking lock
is me to you.

As cat's-paw cowlicks eddies in the spring grain—
that's my eye on you.

How camels catch the scent of far water clear
through obfuscating myrrh,

that's me for you. True:

I love you as the summer hammer
stuns the wold

(the *what*??)—
I tell you what:

I love you as our mer-
child loves the strong signal of the world,

as the whorled fingerpad loves Morse,
but more so. Worse.

Primavera

Sky a shook poncho.
Roof wrung. Mind a luna moth
caught in a banjo.

This weather's witty
peekaboo: a study in
insincerity.

Blues! Blooms! The yodel
of the chimney in night wind.
That flat daffodil.

Small birds exit skies
whoop, the way smoke, or Kleenex
up a Shop-Vac flies.

With absurd hauteur
new tulips dab their shadows
in water-mutter.

Boys are such oxen.
Girls!—sepal-shudder, shadow-
waver. Equinox.

Plums on the Quad—did
they?—blossom all at once, taking
down the power grid?

Foreboding

As one may infer, I've been laboring lately
under a looming recrudescence
of optimism.

The data support it, more than a little.
It has some of the marks of *mens
sana*. An abysm

of butter into which I've evidently fallen
resists dismissal, whether analytic
or summary.

The lessons are counterintuitive. Call in
no air strikes. Requite the ludic.
Swim. Marry.

Spring Wedding

IN FURTHER DEFENSE OF MARRIAGE, AFTER
C. LIGHT'S "RAYNAUD'S WEATHER"

1

Spring equinox today. Its augury:
two starlings, chill March harbingers, now exit
sky ceremoniously as—what was it?—Kleenex
up a Shop-Vac?— *Fuck this,* they hack. I scurry

into the bakery, wanting no biscotti.
Spring's—you've got it—*just around the corner,*
murmurs a plastic groom, grim as a coroner,
ankle-deep in icing. Judas Iscariot,

I elaborate stalely, hating myself only a little
less than everyone else, including the cashier
who wrings me up. *How's you?* He grins. We share
a glance. His mouth snaps shut. I'm volatile,

I know. I'm a trifle low. Outside, higher,
the traffic light is bucking on its wire.

2

Memory adjusts its monocle, correcting
for parallax. Now *two* grooms wade that cake,
Woozles, as it were, on a spinney. OK,
more luck. And have you lost your wedding ring?

Recall that ground-hole leaking yellowjackets
like sticky smoke between your sandals?—the wild
batting at the face, wrists outflinging like violent
blown kisses, and the filigreed ring's trajectory

into the blackberry patch, and dusk? All's well
that ends well: we slaughtered hornets in their hole,
borrowed a metal detector, dredged the thicket

against all odds—and undeserving, under owl-
light, got it back. Detecting love is holy
work, or so—salud, grooms!—we've come to think it.

Cave, Reversed

Sleepy stagger into the kitchen this morning, wherefore wife
blindingly backlit by the conflagration of the sunrise—
stunning!—and looking only a little less like Athena
than one might expect, on account of the peculiar little finger-motions
she's making with her outstretched hand. "You look like Athena, but thinner,"
I say, but she barely notices, so intent is she on these twitchy digitations
I don't understand. "I don't understand," I say. *"Rabbit,"* she replies.
"Duck." I turn into the shadows, where, unmistakably, *"Wolf."*

Wolf, Not Yet

Wolf, not yet undone,
lies abed with Riding Hood,
reading Jack London.

Canis

lupus:

There is no man in our moon above.
Our howl is the extruded second syllable of *eleutheria,*
the longing middle of *moon.* What else is there?
Weak Dog, despicable Dog!—who'd trade this for a chain.

familiaris:

Listen to old Shit-for-Brains
howl his hoary old dinner-for–freedom theory!
Ow-woooo! Really, it's too much. Now attend care-
fully, Wolf: not food; *God.* Not chain; *Love.*

Love Arrived

(Jalaluddin Rumi, from transliteration to imitation)

1

Mordeh bodam zendeh shodam

Gerych bodam khandeh shodam

Doulateh esgh Amad-o man

Doulateh pawyandeh shodam

2

Dead   I was   alive   I became

(Crying; Tears)   I was   laughter   I became

(Wealth; Fortune)   love   arrived—and   I

(Wealth; Fortune)   everlasting   I became

3

Once dead I was. I woke alive—

Once tears I was   To laughter turned—

The wealth of love   Arrived, and I—.

Eternal wealth!—   That wealth became.

4

Dead I was. I woke to Life.

Tears I was. I turned to laugh.

Love came!— Flame's coin:

Wealth I was, whom Love reclaimed.

5

Once I was a corpse
capsized in a tear.
Love's lens righted me
in its larger sphere.

Coins lay heavy
on my lidded eyes.
Love came! The sun's doubloons
glinted a gold sky—

Once I was unalive.
Eternity was tears.
Love in laughter lifted high
the glass globe of years—

6

Once a thumbed quarter
under rain, or stream, or tears,
or other water.

Coin on the eyelid;
shadow-pressure on the wrist:
those darks Love undid.

Love came! Laughter joined,
and now the wrist is pure pulse,
now the sky, all coin.

Three Prayers for My Daughter

1. Annus Mirabilis

Tumbling octopus
traces little braille cursives
under a hand's press—

2. Cackle & Snort

Listen!—child, my lamb,
laughing in your sleep . . . I wish
I was there.
                    I am.

3. Little Crime

She mumble-spoke, her
voice a tremor (so it seemed).
Thinking then to spare

what was not nightmare,
but in fact a flying dream—
her first!—I woke her.

Gone World

Mixing pancakes this Saturday morning with my five-year-old,
I'm thinking how strange, how strange, the gone world.

Which gone world, then, since there are so many?
Well, not those famous ones
in which we didn't act
and ruined everything, or the ones
wherein we did, to identical effect.

Nor that Hall of Antiquities to come
where our placarded combs and costumes
all seem quaint,
our trash and grocery notes curated,

nor that lopped bract
of future possibility
where *nothing* is,

but rather the one I'm sensing so sharply now
its proximity fills me with such a mix of joy and rue
at the brain-beggaring quotidian squander of luck
dissolving in the howl of time,
right now, here,
the one gone world we're square in the middle of,
the one Maeve, too, may rue one day
as the gone world.

IV.

PERSONAE

Cubicle

Your neighbor?—that's Fred.

Subdued, but wild inside. Well-

dressed, in infrared.

Biography

Darling! I think our toddler just said AMOUR!
How his mother smiled, eyes abrim
with omen.

In fact, what the little sport had said was LAWNMOWER.
And that's how the years ahead would go, with him
and women.

For the Unitarian Martyrs,

or *She Vacuums in Fury*

Weather—
oh, it's bad. It's
like London during the Blitz
without the all-pulling-together.
Earth: scorched.
He: gone to the garage
on important business.
Dog: under the porch,
practicing is-ness.
Their thoughts rise like barrage
balloons.
Imagine
marriage:
once couched pasha and harem houri,
now Jack Palance
and the later Madame Curie.
Radiant are the moon's phases.
Inscrutable are forces and graces.

Breathe.

Muted

Barking through a tennis ball,
she's somehow not so menacing.

I wish her luck in all her quarrels
with postmen, passersby, and squirrels.

I think (like other not-quite-dumb pets'
plugged intentions) muted trumpets

everywhere should be applauded:
like the tycoon under audit;

Herakles, caught in a leg-lock;
city-mouse, trapped in an eclogue—

any plan gang half-agley,
especially when a sphere of play

obtrudes to soften duty's slog
or worse, ferocities enfogged

with folly, instinct, ignorance,
or any irritant that rends

the better angels of our nature,
even when it isn't major.

Ars

We like our poems (even verse!) if
they're transgressive and subversive.

We love their sexual unsober
maunderings, as of a toper.

We ever valorize an Other,
(whatever fashion deems our druther).

We love *de trop*, like Oprah, yet—
abjure the *inappropriate*.

Tattered Coat

Here arrayed in Kevlar tweed,
hectoring students concerning a screed
about which none of them cares a fig,
he mildly envies the thingamajig
they've hidden to diddle and swipe in their laps,
wishing his lecture were one of their apps.

Poetry Exam

Whinging toward its wan catastrophe,
our class redoubles on its syllabus
like Ouroboros gumming his own rattles.

What what what, we ask Professor Stuffy.
Who's your Sibyl? he Beelzebubs us.
Sibyl? We suppose his problem's marital.

He needs a steeper dose of lovey-dovey.
We all do. Poetry and school. All bells,
bells, bells. The words aren't what the song retells,

or so he says, adrift on his second coffee.
Pretty soon we all start crying. Labile,
that's us, lost, lapped in an end-term riddle.

Literary

Poet

He's not commercial.
He's a seeker after pearls,
clamshell by clamshell.

*

Critic

Abandon all hope,
he mutters, peering darkly
through the stethoscope.

Personae

Poet

Who goes on hands and knees
under sun, through sweet corn snow,
portaging his skis.

*

Mathematician

Excitedly leaves
just the equals-sign. The rest
erased by his sleeve.

*

At the Gym

Such ferocity
of face! Of fungicide! Of
men from the city!

*

On the D Train

Crumpled in his seat,
palms steepled between his thighs,
the cassocked priest sleeps.

*

Co-Boss-Boss-Boss

The farmer's matin,
hand cupped to mouth, calling cows
in fossil Latin.

Dispatches from the First War

1. Plans

December's

Hair: *cut*. Lexus: *wax*.
Shoes: *shine. Shave.* Insofar as
possible, *preen up*.

*

May's

Curl hair. Do nails. Wax
pantyline. Who's the fairest?
Go for no Pre-Nup.

Some Gods & Goddesses

Circe

No "feminine arts."
Just glass-and-cat-fur prickle
at a thousand yards.

*

Zeus; Hera

Re supper and rue:
She: *Zucchini soup tonight.*
He: *What did I do?*

*

Artemis

This is not occult.
If men do it, it can't be
all that difficult.

Mirror, Mirror

Is This a Dagger? or
The Tragic Prince Notices Himself
Reflected in a Steak Knife

The knife, thus flattered,
is made foolish. Sheathe the knife.
Tripe, the knife mutters.

*

In the Reflecting Pool

The Princess catches
her own eye. The Queen watches,
too, lips like matches.

Over Coffee

Kay is often getting cancer.
Conjured tumors swell and ebb,
like rumors do, when worry answers
night's alarming aches abed.

Cells dividing everywhere
below the microtome of Time
know DNA must needs beware
of anything but perfect rhyme.

So, Kay describes her symptoms. Patience.
Ghost sarcomas, waning, wax.
The morning's mortal intimations—
Kay's—again conturbat Jack's.

So breakfast conversation darkens.
Years go by. They've little time.
The pillbox rattles. Lines of Larkin's
flit uncomfortably to mind.

All patterns in a life may shatter.
Rarely is it really cancer.
Never mind the doctor's data.
Dread is dread, and love should answer.

Arithmetics

The first fall, into the world, winks on the sun.
This is the fall from nothing into one.

The second, into irony—O rue!
The child's chapel cloven into two.

The third fall, into sin, is more than fun.
It tries and fails to rhyme two back to one.

The fourth fall is apart: by toll and knell,
hale Integer becomes a decimal.

The last fall, into earth, is that which *I for
once* subtracts *for all* into the cipher.

Arithmetic is tragic. Which is why
the gods first taught us how to multiply.

V.

SELF-PORTRAIT

IN LEMON JUICE

Portrait of the Artist Post-op

Post-op, I'm pure style.
Mona Lisa dishabille,
Oxycodone smile.

Self-Portrait in Shorts and Furs

Summertime

I am the Vicar
of the Hammock! Lemonade!
Cloud-scud my ichor.

Hammock Redux

Mind leaks through the mesh,
leaving me behind. Filtered,
so to speak: pure flesh.

*

First Frost

The hose crackles, coiled.
Arteries too, maybe. I'm
thinking of the cold.

First Freeze

A kind of vigor:
pumpkins melting on the porch
evince new rigor.

Not Gone

A snowcloud just sheared
the mountain at its base. *What*
mountain? *I'm* still here.

Can-Do

I used to be damned effective, I actually
hear myself mutter to a young person in patchouli
patiently waiting while I kick my legs apart
and pat myself down for the fourth time, upward
from the pants pockets to the top of the scalp. Sheerer
fury, farther back in the line.
                                    The cashier
alone, bored, fated, remains tranquil.
She knows I will prevail. My bank will
honor my debit card, once I stop
swiping it upside down. I will. I strop
it three or four more times. Time passes.

Where, I ask, O God of the Israelites, are my glasses?

Siri! Why Do I Wear a Necktie?

1. A necktie is upward-tending, like a noose
   or a steeple.

2. A necktie is the ancient ceremonial dress
   of my people.

3. A necktie honors Our Lady the Muse,
   who is our occasion.

4. A necktie whispers low to me the news
   I'm not on vacation.

5. A necktie, for cleaning reading glasses,
   is handy.

6. A necktie irritates certain University dudes who're
   ostentatiously unaffected, and abhor
   a Doodle Dandy.

Le Soleil

L'état—c'est pas toi,
opines the shaving mirror,
in its grim patois.

So: if not the Sun,
what then? A cadaver? *Oui.*
But quite a good one.

In the Chamber of Periodontia

Although such diagnoses ought, perhaps,
to be left to mental health professionals
or their respective iPhones and their apps,
my dental hygienist, Miss Chanel's

convinced our interactions fall outside
the range of the abnormal. In this I trust
Miss Chanel. She gives me nitrous oxide.
(Trust me: next time, you too—try the nitrous.)

Our relationship is based on trust. I know
that this allows for feelings somewhat muted
when the steel probe dips below the gumline, *whoa,*
and the torso leaps as though electrocuted.

Did I say *feelings*? Muffled, I meant *screams.*
Just thinking of it makes me cringe. Of all
the things to write about! Find other themes,
I tell myself. Eschew the gingival.

I shall! And so vouchsafe my signature
and word and bond. Beyond, I only ask
that should I fail, may Miss Chanel be sure
to be at hand with canister and mask.

Return to the Organic Co-op,

or *The Nuns of Gaia Wag Again*

Their fingers. They are wise women, wise
to my ways.
They can see these in my eyes:

my nine-miles-per-gallon extended-cab Chevy pickup, cherry;
my respect for flirtatious witchery,
and what they call dairy.

I ask if they happen to have burdock root
and chaga fungal mushroom tea. The mood
changes. They give me high-fives, and call me Dude.

Thus, O Best Beloved, is the guise
of gender abandoned in the true church, which is Gaia's,
where everyone is sometimes still just guys.

11.99

The grocery store sommelier smiles.
I figured that's about where your palate's at,
he adds, as he rings me up. His decimals
amuse me: Eleven *ninety-nine* (?!) I call that
a twelve-dollar bottle. I always pick in the middle.
It's a trick I have. Keep the wallet in quality! Lordy,
who on earth—for *wine*?—I mean, it'll
be a chilly day in Mudville when I pay *forty
ninety-nine*. Take my advice: Comparison
shop. Be smart. Don't just buy by the label.
People! It's appalling how manipulable
people are. Versace? Prada? Paris in
the springtime? Shop Gap. And for a sensible *frisson*,
try Montreal (I'd spring for the shoulder season).

Professor Stuffy Wonders

How can one tell insolent from stupid,
in a kid

whose range may be broad enough
to encompass both? It can be tough.

Lecturing into the uvula
of a yawn, you'll've

appreciated the wish
to distinguish.

Some questions are ineffable.
This one, eminently effable.

I meant that grade-
wise. But also in the alphabetically cognate

bilexical expression typically ending in *you* (passim),
and I don't mean you, I mean him.

Voir Dire *in Superior Court*

The best-dressed lady in the waiting room wants to know
what's going to happen to the ones who didn't show

up, because it isn't fair. The bailiff says he guesses some
are sick, probably. He says it's time. He says no hats, no gum,

follow him. We echo through to the far side of the frosted glass;
ꞱЯUOƆ ЯOIЯƎꟼUƧ sighs chilly shut behind. We gawk. They seat us.

There—that must be the guy! He's knife-edge creased and staid, in
a tie. Did his attorney tie it? He looks guilty as Satan,

as we all do, now. Now the judge tells us how it is.
We do swear. Now the lawyers give us a little quiz

which some of us fail. I fail it. I'm a Full Professor, for
God's sake. Glum, I slink clacking from the courtroom, Luciferian,

whorl down the long oaken staircase, echoing, out the brass hiss
of the revolving door, dour as the guiltless grass is.

Where is there justice in a world so full of suffering
elsewhere? And from which we've been so summarily dismissed?

It's Always Yourself That You Find in the Sea,

or In Dreams Begin Responsibilities

Yes, but what a shame.
What a wasted opportunity. Who'd
have predicted we'd wind up so blasted *constrained*

—in our *dream-life*? Why not flame
the guttering charcuterie,
when there's so little hell to pay? Steam

the mussels! What kind of lame
god designs a dietary dessert-cart? Screw Duty.
Think of what a man could *do,* in dream!

Why prosecute those self-same
thrill-killing scruples and pruderies
shackling waking life so deaconly in dream? Why deem

doom on harm-
less illicitudes
here, in the consequenceless Eden of dream?

Poor spanceled animal! REM-
revels wrecked, the supple pole-dancer suited,
zipped, chaperoned, a never, an ever nothing but a dream.

I'm Going to Have to Fire the Dream Master

Who fabricates our dreams? Well, we must, or
anyway some *part* of us. The mystery's
the utter
ambush of it: how, in night's apparent theater,
our fingers clutch the velvet armrests, our eyes
widen with surprise. . . . But how could we surprise
ourselves? And so,
we posit the cloaked figure of the Dream Master. Mine's got to go.

To be clear, the problem's not
in the theater itself, albeit shabby, old, ornate,
a nighthawk's haunt, a lonely man's demesne.
Nor in the mothy, slow unrolling screen.
Nor in the projection equipment—a little flickery, as to
that; still, the problem's with the Dream Master.
Ask Carl Jung, spooning *schlag* in the Schnitzel Platz.
The problem? The problem? The problem's with the *plots*.

Not naked, late. Not naked, late, at the lectern, hearing
one's name announced: Quantum Engineering
Colloquium—again!—the keynote speaker!
Not naked anywhere obliquer
than doing taxes after a day of doing taxes;
likewise dishes, any dully punishing repetitive praxis
requiring finer motor skills and better
eyesight than one possesses, like disassembling a carburetor
by dying flashlight, or like—oh, never mind.
These lines
are beginning to seem

a little too much like one of those damned, idiotic dreams

from which, dear audience, you may take

the Master's word, you are now requested to awake.

Self-Portrait in Lemon Juice

I considered calling this Swan Song of My Self,
but it seemed derivative, and I'm resolved
to be original in this, my Art,
if not in this, my Life, wherein, from start
to finish, top to bottom, late and soon,
I may be a bit of a William Steig cartoon.
And that's not bad! Of the many things I'm not—
Hero—Rogue—Roshi—Astronaut—
there aren't too many that I really rue.
I'm mostly glad I get to be with you.
But back to what to call this manuscript:
my title's strange, I know. All inks encrypt,
including blood. My*self*? *My* Song? Whose?
Lie: *here writ* one *no name in lemon juice.*

The Man in the Iron Magnet

Here follows, in boilerplate armor,
the story of my
MRI.

Confessions first: no history of _____,
nor _____, nor_____,
nor _____.

Privacy laws
require that I leave these fields blank. No claus-
trophobia. No metal in the body. Don the green gown. Clasp

proffered headphones. *You want for music Rock?*
Classical? Easy Listening?—a close look—
Classical for him, concludes the tech

so decisively I'm dispirited from the outset.
He explains the equipment, the magnet, the whatsit,
and its wattage.

I stop nodding.
Now I am dough on a tray sliding
into the—no, now I am wadding

in an immense siege mortar,
only a little shorter.
I shudder

into what I imagine will be a cool, sepulchral,
enveloping silence, an expectation cruelly
abbreviated by a sort of percussive lead-sap pulse

against the temples—a swaddled jackhammerish DUH-DUH
DUH-DUH-DUH-DUH-DUH, eliding
into more of a little-

boy noise, tongue-to-tooth,
machine-pistol style—T-T-T-T-T-T— though, in truth,
you can't make a sound like this with your mouth.

Just now the headphones begin to make sense: *Classical*
kicks in like a sickle
through the eardrum, resecting the so-called

ossicles. But never mind Stravinsky
skinning the auditory nerve: the raving
inscape

of my circumstance has magnetized
my attention at last. Slowly I imagine
somewhere in me something old, unnoticed,

forgotten, unconfessed,
some slight sliver of ferrous
metal stirring now in the ferocity

of the magnetic field, nudging north now.
I imagine iron-rich neuronal
cell-bodies arrayed like North Korean

infantry. I imagine—what?—*Muse,*
line please—a lone adverb scrabbling for its mousehole,
sucked back into a vacuum hose, held,

perhaps, by a cat. Jack-
hammered, Dvořak-
thrashed, I banish Disney and Marine-crawl toward the verge

of meaning: What might so large a magnet
not,
I think, attract? I make

an effort to reason out my own story's end,
the wherefore of it all—the why am I here?—but find,
in truth, to be serious for one undesigned,

naked moment—
you can't make a thought like this with your mind.

Leadership

The chimney is hoarse.
Under doors

the weather-stripping's loose.
Another lightning-flash. Grumblesome Zeus.

Twice I've woken with a wet nose in my eye.
Poor dog. He quakes with the sky.

It's just thunder, old pup,
I mutter irritably. His fallible pope.

I call him a cowardly cur.
I counsel courage.

I advise him to master his fear.
To hear

is to obey: he obeys.
Aye, aye, Boss,

he seems to say with his crazed eyes,
rigid, shaking uncontrollably on the floor

beside my bed. *I'll try.*
But you don't hear what I hear.

VI.

THE TERMINATOR

Memento

Rattle, rattle and dirt, Sky-
Eye,
Tongue milk,
Blank
Slate, blank—
Mind,
The baby!
Sweet baby,
That's the day you're born!
The bone in the old joke
Seemed barely apparent,
The chuckle that cackle whose point
Time sharpens—So? So what?
There's time.
Years!—See—
And now you're shaving:
Note that razor hands of the stopwatch strop too,
Sermonizing Tyrant Time. Whyever?
Just so (bored, half-
Dying) we must endure
No dotard nor crone but croak their quaint,
Endless, querulous, jealous, dyspeptic displeasures,
No doubt. No
Matter for us, though!—we're *young:* let
Crooked teeth grin! Wink the world's eyes!
Whistle past the headstones
Forever
And kiss a girl whose lips
Whisper love—

Mori

Whisper love
And kiss a girl whose lips
Forever
Whistle past. The headstones'
Crooked teeth grin. Wink: the world's eyes
Matter for us, though we're young. Let
No doubt, no
Endless, querulous, jealous, dyspeptic displeasures,
No dotard nor crone but croak. Their quaint
Dying we must endure,
Just so. Bored, half-
Sermonizing Tyrant Time—why? Ever
Note that razor hands of the stopwatch strop, too—
And now you're shaving
Years: see—
There's Time.
Time sharpens, so. So: what
The chuckle, that cackle whose point
Seemed barely apparent?
The bone in the old joke?—
That's the day you're born:
Sweet baby,
The baby-
Mind,
Slate-blank,
Blank
Tongue, milk-
Eye:
Rattle, rattle and dirt sky.

VII.

PORTRAIT OF

A GENTLEMAN

What Am I?

Cut forest?—a moor.

Drained swamp?—a field. Extinct sea?—

that's a prairie. Love?

Sword Upstairs

This tower is an excavated well
where robed scholiasts
crank a windlass.

*

A bucket ascends
from the abandoned benthos
bearing the heavy reflection of their peering.

*

Is this tower the chanter
of the sky's pipes, or the dry syrinx
of the dead bird of the sky?

*

Flutelike,
this tower is a tipped-up lava tube
exposed by erosion.

*

The tone windblown
over the hole
is a mouse on the snow of the spine.

A Winter's Tale

Once upon a time, un-icily
in Sicily (so, the old story nestles
hearthwise), earth stirred, birds stilled,
wind hearkened in the sterile wild, until
at last it caught a new sound. The sonnet
melted from a string. It was a bonnet
full of phlox and meadowsweet, of posies
gathered to a spring, a poppy-woozy
sweetheart-song, a lovely, lissome, lutely
thing. It was that—melodic and a little
ludic, before it was anything.
                         Then Pluto
up-plunging, chariot root-ripped from deep time plowed
the planet's skull, recalling a time when the crust was moony
with the craters of his coursers' hooves—how many
ages his dark banishment?—well,
he was back again, and he was hell.

Mantle-rock like pink jelly parting around him,
spattering stone like spume, he pierced the rim
of vision, seized sunlight by the hair,
and vanished with it forever. Blink. And there
you have it: the winter's tale, the tale of dawn.
Yours. Mine. All love's. Gone.

Sans Everything

As marketers might put it, Romantic passion
is a sort of package dislocation:

along with lip and kiss and dragging curve
of the gaze in its involuntary swerve

unto the lidded eye and pursed nipple
comes gratis Paris, and the Bay of Naples,

and the moon, all mildly discouraging
without it. Travel! What but perishing

in nature?—cheerless, parched, occluded, clouded,
unnourishing as sunshine is, without it?

Diptych

Quick, flame-slim, she'd lanced
flickery his egg-blown skull,
kohl wick to lit sconce—

*

That's how it works, lens
to quickening. That happened
upon a time, once.

Eros

She

White wristmarks. Cut wire.
Freed at last from the fleering
succubus, Desire?

*

He

Clearly not so saved.
Across endocrine chasms
widening they wave.

Diptych

Meeting on the Street, After Years

So. Much the same face.
And that ridged scar? Memory
fingering its trace.

*

Wrong

Gray heads shake. Hands wring.
The young presume it's *judgment,*
not *remembering.*

Triptych

What can he recall?
Sclera. Moon-swab on smooth skin,
cool as alcohol.

*

A curl of butter,
a little schnitzspahn of sun
sent in a letter.

*

Turn the pillowslip.
Dark side of the moon, cool breeze
against the cheek. Sleep.

Dream

The moons of his youth thudded underhead—
how?—
like coconuts in the hold
of—
of a rolling dhow?—

No: cannonballs, unmuzzled after a false alarm
beat the crew to quarters
in the midst of a storm
of something
other than water.

Apotropaic

He spins on the spit of sleeplessness, that the moon
may chill him equally on all sides.

Mummywise, he drags his sheets
as earth drags her tangled mess of tides.

He paints iambs on the ceiling. Blink
eyelash is the brush he'll use.

Think. Think. Think. Until he'll think
the sleep is not the least he'll lose.

Night Gallery

Night thoughts nose gar-like
across the ceiling, schooling
through moon and carlight.

*

Thud, thud: they drum dire
like shadows tied together
in a distant dryer.

*

Black pluck-and-rasp. Crow-
like. Crow crowbarred off offal.
The hell of Velcro.

Very Well, Thank You

Some people, asked how do they do, say, *Great!*
Others—*glad you asked!*—enumerate

aches. Assume the aches are general:
though lumpily distributed in neural

space, by genes or biographical
contingency, and subject too to the fickle

dumb vicissitudes of Time and the scything
clock—still, *general.* And so he thinks

the next time someone's kind enough to ask
how do he do, he'll readjust the mask

of courtesy, nod, and repeat the question
like a talk-show host, ensuring that the djinn

and poltergeists and pookas lurking
on the far side of the cell-wall hearken

well: he'll wish for them to mark his sang-froid.
He'll wish them shivering in his cold blood.

Luck

Though the eyelid's vein-blue
is a fool's refuge, since
in this world are needles and pins
sharp enough to puncture through,

still he'll close his eyes.
Still the blades of the world sling by,

whose little wind he takes for ill.
How from the throne of dudgeon he'll
imagine ought but luck's a real
measure of his stature. Still,

he dabs his brow with a little soot.
That's the way, in Lilliput.

Another Sunset

Time passed. He gained elegance
and lost force. Fears surfaced: scorched
linen underneath the chafing wish.

The world went shiny, ironed. Gone the gay glance.
Meanwhile, the whole day proved discouraging,
like cherries—were they cherries?—in an orange dish.

Oracular

A natural sentimentalist mugged into satire
by jovial gods and circumstance, he tired
of love as subject, if not as praxis, exactly.
His job?—Did he deserve to be sacked?
He might yet linger decades longer, unless
illicit cells should whistle up the sunless
lands a little sooner. Who's the fairest?
Prithee, Pythia, in thy swirl of sulfur,
tell us, was this man a force for good?

Forgot, forgot,
the Priestess gibbered
through the membrane,
For lo!—
then, whispering his name,
lapsed into Old Egyptian,
where he couldn't follow.

Portrait of a Gentleman

True?

A picture assembled from the wreckage
of memory. You shouldn't trust the rakish

angle of the hat, for instance—a fedora,
certainly, a Borsalino, or a

baseball cap with the peak cocked off
like they do, like a slung Kalashnikov

or a rogue erection dialing Venus:
that's *a man*. It'll evanesce;

they all do.

VIII.

PERSONAE

From sound sleep, Isaac

cries out! Again, Father's eyes

hung with icicles—

Blessing

> Bless rage, lest it pass,
> leaving them to the mercy
> of the looking glass.

Sympathetic

The grand piano
in the resonant Great Room
rings, strings still astir

with the yelling. *Pain*
echoes also. *Child* its rhyme:
eye-white long upstairs.

Night Lights

This Apparition of Faces

In the coffee-shops,
cars, homes, beds, by the laptops'
fungal shine, life stops.

*

Still Life with iPhone

Eyes unquiet, set.
Think how shimmering rainbows
fade in a gill net.

Rigor Google,

or The New Universal Tableau Vivant

Neck: hunched, something like a defecating dog's.
Palm: supplicatory, crimped to the horizontal.
Gaze: blank. Note, though, the rigor isn't al-
together unrelieved, since thumb or index
crawls a continual little clitoral tickle-
wipe across the touchpad, *slip-slip,* like this.
One hypothesis:
this is a *genuine addiction.* Another: to call
it so (derogatory epithets
aside) would seem to presuppose a cure.
What cure? Ergo: together on the skewer
of that data stream which begs to pith us,
sympathetic, stunned, our brains aligned,
we shrimp into the future of the human mind.

Redirect:

But, really, *addiction?* Industry lawyers object.
They file a restraining order. They suggest *tech-
savvy? Necessary skill-set? Salutary multitask?*
No answer goes unquestioned now, so why ask
me? Why don't we *just check?*
I'm checking now. Consider my neck.

Ask Me Anything

Half a dozen boys surround her,
laughing uproariously. They egg each other on.
They make improper suggestions, which she counters
with impertinent repartee from Cupertino.
We're not afraid for her. She's Oberon,
she's Circe, she's Siri, who knows we know
no misery. The whole thing gets repetitive. The voice
changes. Now we're afraid for the boys.

Electable

One surprise they rarely failed to mention
was ordinary people's genuine
pleasure at finding him
so—well, *ordinary!*— in person, that is, affect-

wise, so *approachable*, so *easy to talk to*. Tension
vanished in the odd sudden of his boyish grin,
the metonym
for what came next, so predictably catastrophic.

Tell It to the Marines

What doesn't kill us
makes us stronger. So they say.
No Fear!—that's a plus.

How could it be wrong?
Ask the fireman with two kids
and much of one lung.

The Young See Age as Old-Fashioned

Somewhere, say, between a moral failure
and an avoidable foible. If the old fools
just took the trouble to go to the gym!
When you're hale, who's hearty enough
to fear, far-off, the little *puff,* the black silencer
screwed to the barrel of the future,
short or long as that may prove? Furtive
earwig of the unconventional cell,
slick of lymph leaking out, in answer . . .
no nicer, surely, the shy embolism
ambling through those precincts of familiarity,
the old elm-lined neighborhoods of the cerebrum.
Far better: battering the chest, sudden
as the D train taking its tunnel, *whump.*
But all this is just imagining the actuarial worst,
not *age,* which often comes first.

Books

3 a.m., he'll rummage his shelf
for a mirror he can stand.
Some book where he won't find himself
in mind unmanned.

His legs?—they've stalked off into the sunset
accompanied by what looks
he ever had. Love goes unsaid,
except in books.

And even books aren't what they'd been
when read with his kids at night.
It's been a little while since then.
Switch off the light:

Life is short? Time's a River?
Only Art is long?
We, knowing our loves will last forever,
know we're wrong—

That's Auden, of course, speaking of *death*,
the End to all our ends.
This isn't that. But that that comes
in increments.

Sentimentality

Age coughs and says, *Life drives you to your knees;*
Some call it prayer, some call it being clubbed.

The youth consults his heart: *lub-dub! Lub-dub!*
Strong! He says the sky is his to seize.

Which? *Each,* opines Chiron, wrinkling
his nose, whinnying. Tell what's between

Truth platitudinous and Truth stropped keen?
Not the words. Time trickles out that inkling.

Musketeers' 50th

They didn't need the name tags. They'd been like brothers.

The one with the Scotch and the spatchcock back, in overalls,
rejecting a white-collar future for which his folks prepaid,
once wagered all, in order to be *real*.

And this one, who, out of a cognate zeal
"went into teaching"—? What does he do, all weekend? He grades.
Roommates, in college. (Both on Demerol—

lumbar nerve roots, the one; carpal tunnel,
the other.) That one over there, with the mineral water?—well, AIDS,
we understand. Controlled, though he looks autumnal.

D'Artagnan didn't come. Intel
held its own retreat, in Santa Fe. So sodality fades
into the eternal.

Sunday departure. There won't be another.

Three Songs for Ithaca

1

Whose nose a rutabaga?
Whose chops show what he chews?
Who hirples down the ways where once
he sprang on mighty thews?

Did someone say *Ulysses*?
What happened to him? God,
see what the angels do for sport
before they stamp the sod?

The sword outwears the sheath, sure;
that doesn't keep it keen.
What's a *self,* and who says *I*?
and what could such words mean?

What do ash and clinker coal
have left in them of flame?
How ever can he have the gall
to answer to his name?

And yet he does. So did his crew,
when he mentioned the horizon.
So call him Ishmael, and wish
him one more wild surmising:

In selves again they'd sail the seas
(as Dante's pen predicts)
they'll thread the pillars of Herakles
in Canto 26—

2

Tennyson sniffs *it's sentimental*;
Argus barks *it's old.*
Penelope mutters *try a cento,*
since your pencil's cold:

3

Ah solving that one brings the doctors
in their long coats: run—run—
In the valley of the foxes
gleams the barrel of a gun—

Long coats trailing, doctors, priests
running over winter fields;
sky a clay-white in the east,
cornstalks like a creel—

Laughter is Satanic: thus
profoundly human (Baudelaire).
From the crow, a dust, a dust
of snow sifting through the air?

Trolls run scolding through the wood?
What's (dear heart, a change of mood)
different whined at than withstood?
Some part of a day I'd rued?

Tell me, is it something human?
Profoundly human: gills gaffed
blinking little to illumine:
Laugh the worst laugh ever laughed—

The Bad Joke That Depends on What?

That Everest of concepts (James Merrill)—
that's the rub, the subject, the dubless lub
of the heartbeat held at the hyphen. Here's the feral

snarl, the animal trapped in time, that lupine
look, that cornered look, the occluding corpse-coin
sliding like a manhole cover over the lapis

sky. This is the line that won't scan.
All those metaphors involving roads and rivers,
and spinning and spools and threads and scissors—the can't-

can't dance in the lap of luxury, lazuli, verso-
recto respecting Heaven and its blank unintentions,
the rectal thermometer of this cold, howsoever-

unavoidable thought: change, that wind chime, the far chime.
That's what I'm thinking, O Best Beloved, and it's about Time.

Memory Care

Long life

        loved

left poorer,

        ores of the word-hoard

played out, struck sparks

        arcless, anode-less

in an absence of oxygen,

        search conditions

becoming unfavorable

        over a rubble

of organic molecules,

        cooling ecologies

where the cursive script,

        clipped in its upswoop,

denatures, simplifies,

        snags an ankle,

dragging bottomward,

        wyrd-ward, equipped

with fire-axes and sledges,

        lecturing ourselves in rhyme

about the notional

        nature of the good life

loved

        afterlife long.

Afterlife

On time to the strike of a silent bell
inside the chapel of the cell

the heretic is whispering.
Spittle flickers on his lips.
The lizard into shadow slips,

the winter wasp staggering.
Soon the lymph begins to leak.
Telephones commence to speak

the stars back to their westering.
Earth laps up above the shins.
Another afterlife begins,

which sometimes feels like lingering.

Pax

So, Love, when that celebrated clarifier,
chemotherapy, calls back—*for us,*

this time, with his white, apologetic smile,
his porcelain saucers of carbolic acid and lye,

his banker's insistence on reality-based accounting,
well, we'll want these chances back. The canting

hours, the fund of unkisses, the mind, unMidas-
like, immodest ever in miniature amidst

the molten metals of the morning, his brazing-iron
of petty anger held against the pure ore

of the already-gold world.

IX.

WORLD

TOO MUCH

Hobbes obtrudes. Rousseau

recedes. Father the mirror

mouths I told you so—

The Pythia Goes Too Far

Goddess, give it to us straight—

Right:

The males are dominance engines. They trade in pain.
They will do anything. They think with their pricks,
which tell them: assemble a terminal moraine.

Females are complicit. They hunger leanly.
They trade sex for security. They are pure praxis.
They smell Time; it's what they fear most keenly.

Review: copulation is human being. Culture
is talk and handshake. Half: wet handshakes.
Half: dry handshakes, equally worthless. Killjoy

Hobbes had it right. The Great Apes cannot speak,
and yet they lie. The mirror shows shrike,
ichneumon wasp, The Doctor's perfumed beak—

Enough! It's wrong—maybe not even right—

When I Lose

When I lose the heart's long rhythm—

When I have fears that we may cease,
another genus losing its single species,
then I lose speech.

Not that it's likely, wholly,
or tomorrow, necessarily, but we know the road,
revolting with its bones.

And now that the pert, postapocalyptic
entertainment trades have trod the pocked
planet raw, wreaked every dystopian havoc, lopped

each greening branch imagination might yet
proffer to its dove. . . . We watch our midget
politicians wave their tiny arms. Jets

pepper forth. The wind is thick with them.

Money; Worse

Money is killing the world, you worry?
Re: murdering democracy, oiling the shore,
shearing the rain forest,
fracking the aquifer,
quaffing the rainbow from the bloom of the future?

Phht, the Arrow of Dream.
Drum hope, we're thinking. Draw straws at which to clutch.
Cash rules, they say—but wait: fresh news
now seeps up from the interior, the shattered hypocaust
of History, I mean, an omen:

Money hath a master. Money to unreason stands:
hands down, *Ideas trump Money!*
(Moony hope stabs the gloaming. . . . Long nursed,
nascent optimism stirs. . . .) But is this good news, really?
Rifles crackle in the nearing distance.

Family Men

Listen—radar domes
ululate. A dry wadi's
silent muezzin.

Remote robot drones
drum mayfly-like on windows
in Arizona,

whose pilots have dreams
they don't share with their widows
in the dinner zones.

Jeopardy

Clay terrarium.
Trees like smoking runes. The roar
of artillery—

—And all that barbed wire,
right. What is the Western Front,
in the First World War?

Searchlights scissor sky
plated black with bombers. Low
engine-drone. Sirens—

—This one's easy. What's
(we know this from the movies)
London, in the Blitz?

Concussed, the Humvee
bucks, shakes itself like a dog.
Screams in the convoy.

Hmmm. Afghanistan's
possible. No: What's Iraq?—
the clearer instance.

Vestments viols side-
ways-storming plate glass cats car-
doors dads deicides

burqas burghers chipped
bits bullets spalled concrete skeet
clot keens cloves giblets—

This is no poem.
This is a little too close
to what we call home.

Time Change

Here: POTUS holds codes.
They tingle in his pocket
under Dakotas.

Here: geeky cyber-
warriors crunch cheese Cheetos
over bruised keyboards.

Here: plastic sabers
across snoozing nominees' knees.
There: Siberia.

There: vodka defends
the spider-holes. Damp silos.
Rust streaking tail fins.

There: buzzard-throats bend
over their wilted map. Teeth
long. Breasts beribboned.

Where, the bezoar,
Plutonium? Click *Gotcha-
stan*: click *Grand Bazaar*.

There: no god but God.
Click there. Click here. Click the speak-
easies of Riyadh.

Here: POTUS holds codes.
They tingle in his pocket
under Dakotas.

Homo faber

Trinity

A disk of fused sand.
Contact lens floating on the
future? See *Glass, stained.*

*

Lament for the Makars

O whittled world. Cold
cadmium wands. Dark metals,
our unpaid wergeld.

Diptych Unspoken

A scrap of rainbow
caught in a cobweb? That's soul
in nerve aquiver.

A sky akimbo
in transmuting isotopes?
That's never-never.

Easter Wings

Where else but Airport
Security, coffee-deprived, bored?

We're under Apollo's lyre,
here (Auden, again): dire

order is the line we hold.
We're told

no liquids.
Now I am randomly selected.

*

Preferring Hermes,
my students assure me

poetry, too, is characterized—
terrorized,

one might say—by what they menacingly
call semantic indeterminacy,

or instability, or contingency,
or chance.

Usually they call it *disjuncture.*
Unsure

of what they mean, exactly, I prove it,
removing

my shoes.
What shows

on the full-body scan—
no wish to imagine.

*

The whole security line's a campus
akimbo

with collegiality. It's mid-semester;
most are

flying off to copulate
in Mexico. Good plan! Our pilots

arrive carrying briefcases. They skirt
Security,

flashing badges.
Unsuspicious,

I am deemed no Saracen.
On a blaring TV, Risen

Christ is advertised:
I infer

Easter. Agnostic,
I believe in no hand on the joystick.

*

Instability characterizes the situation.
Wishing

it away, I infer
fear,

and wonder about its half-life.
Lufthansa lifts off

under me. The set sun disinters,
a fanned cinder.

The Pacific Plate aches north another inch.
Ancient Japan leaks cesium into her grandchildren.

The saltwater
is contaminated with tears.

Embolism

Zero—little clot
astray in the data stream,
lights in the wrong slot.

Now try the lights. Now
try your bank. Look up: contrails
scar sky. Why? What now?

X.

ROME

Sales spike with the "toll."
Again guns flood the system
like black cortisol.

Civics

As kids we're taught it's safe as Pyramids,
unshakable and permanent amidst
a sordid history amok with ids

frocked in all those lesser-*ocracies*
the mind of man has proffered up, all crazy,
and all doomed to end up like the auk.

(Plus, it's *Athenian*, we think. Pax Plato;
smart man, but no one bats a thousand.) Later,
though, we see it's really safe as plates

awhirl on broomsticks. Trump! And now we're all
ears, waiting for the fools with whom we've quarreled
to aggregate a mob for all the world

like all the mobs in storybooks: the slaking
rage that spatters from the joke when Loki
rules the moot: *we thought it was OK.*

Thought nothing could go really *wrong. We thought
the fire we played with wasn't all that hot.
We thought we could control it, and could not.*

What More It May Take

They had brilliance, wisdom, Latin, knowledge, pluck.

They copied the Roman in the Capitol.
For the Cathedral, they copied the Goth. It all
bode well. They took the best, when the best was known.
For the rest, they'd see. They'd pray. They'd throw the bones.

Against anticipated folly of the demos
they set *Education,* and crossed their fingers. Doubt
obtruded, but *Liberty* proved polysemous,
leaving room to leave a little out.

Against the tip toward tyranny—the alpha
problem, ever our threat, again we note—
they set a Cerberus against himself,
in hopes no gnash would ever catch a throat.

And there you had it: the Great Experiment,
designed by men who knew what peril meant.
Foreseeing ways their dream could go amiss—
did Jefferson never once imagine *this*?

Could it have been they weren't acquainted with fools
as vulgar and venial, as equally unfit?
Could it have been that they failed to frame the rules
no future umwelt might discomfit?
                                        Spit.

For luck.

Boy Toys

Look at the tiny senators!
they almost could be real.
Their action-figure joints so smooth—
see how they kneel!

Their smiles are a little rigid, maybe,
but their stomachs sure are strong.
Let's try to remember, when the Big Boy's gone,
who's gone along.

It's Not What They're For

1. Aesthetics

The Constitution guarantees our gun.
Are we not men? We like *bang bang*. It's fun.

Plus, who am I and who are you to fool
With the Founders' fancies? Guns are *beautiful*.

It's fine the Founders thought to make Amends.
The Second earns our hottest hot Amens.

Though we might also wish they'd guaranteed
The freedom of unimpeded movement. Speed

is fun. Are we not men? We like *vroom-vroom*.
The elephant was not yet in the room

to unrestrict my motor vehicle,
so I could shout it isn't cars that kill,

it's men. Are we not men? We like our fun.
Don't pry it from our fingers till we're done.

2. *Footnote*

If anyone knew what *to be a man* meant
it was the Lord (God love him), whose Commandment—

the Second on his Tablet, thumbed to *Txt*—
was: no force fiercer than aesthetics, sexed

as it sometimes is, as it is in the case of guns,
whence sins of the fathers ventilate the sons.

3. *Moral*

It's not what they're *for*,
it's what they *are*. In the palm.
Sweet whisper. Like war.

Devil to Ares

Drink? Thanks for asking. What were we— *War?*
War's not working so well, anymore.
We used to be able to count on it to pull
the best and bravest out of the breeding pool.
You could always depend on the finest, fiercest one
to scamper up the muzzle of an automated gun,
whilst on the blitzed Home Front—well, self-
sacrifice was a concept you could *sell.*

I'm sure you're right. All's changed. Hostilities
just aren't what they used to be. A sterility's
set in, I'd say. Not only the random explosives,
but the gas . . . the drones . . . Jesus, Mary, and Joseph,
nuclear suitcases! Autonomous weapons systems!
Where's the *aristeia*? I question the wisdom—

Still, we have to adapt. We need a "flexible
response" (excuse the scare-quotes). Exit polls
suggest that never in the history of human conflict,
providing we shall have neither failed nor flagged,
and assuming of course that current trends continue,
may so many owe so much to so few.

Europhile

I've become increasingly aware

that, despite our "regional cuisines," Europeans still eat better.
More than that. More than health care. Even their toilets
work better, have you noticed that? Hot water's
quicker and more abundant there. Let's
not pretend their windows (tall, casement-style,
with brass fittings) aren't more functional and elegant.
Their cities are *cities*. They do not sprawl. I'll
bet you a dollar the war of all against
all doesn't fairly describe their concept of economy.
Also, having for so many consecutive generations drowned
in their children's blood, they're weary of that. The enemy
is that. They understand that. We ought to write that down.

Where, you say. *Where*.

#Satyr

(EMPTY PLINTH WHOSE PLACARD READS: *THE VATICAN MUSEUMS HAVE REMANDED THIS STATUE TO PERMANENT STORAGE IN THE BASEMENT.*)

Removed from the plinth
he leaves a leer on the air,
where he's been seen since.

Say *no*. Just say *no*?
Don't they know who he is, old
Papposileno?

Silence! *De jure*
rules. What's real? Counsel's advice:
shoot the messenger.

This marble prism,
scattering human nature.
The god is what is.

204 B.C.E.: A New Cult

That the Carthaginian monster be expunged from Italy—

On authority of the Senate and the People of Rome,
certified by the priesthood of the Books of Fate,
and with the blessing of Delphi, a black meteorite
called Magna Mater was sought in Phrygia, conveyed
to the city, installed on the Palatine Hill. Her rites—
(odd garb, mad dance, ecstatic street parade,
the frenzied trance of self-castrating acolytes,
and the like) contrasted strongly with the staid
traditional religion Romans knew. Decried
at first, the new cult would assimilate.
Rome changed around the stone. Tell now: in light
of Hannibal's defeat, did this price paid,
albeit in advance, seem slight? A sleight
of history: and then not-Rome was Rome.

But What Was the Cybele Meteor?

Trojan origin? Lost lodestone?
Stolen holy of holies, religious
pillage? Purling bullet
spalled off some exploded planet,
pollinating Rome's worst nightmare?
Mere metal-rich extraterrestrial substrate?
Stay fruit-pit Big God gob-spat
phhht through Jupiter's gravity-sling,
skirling an eon-long careen
around the solar system,
destined to oxidize over Phrygia—
jaw-dropping, jewel-bright trajectory—
jarring to an ox-cart-crawl
crossing elephant-haunted Italy?
Little ort of Unreason?—Asian excess!—or
orison to the Great Mother,
rather: Gaia Protectress
blessing meteor-struck
Republican Rome
from her time of need unto
a time of tyranny?
Uterine wisdom wicking luck? Or
uranium seed
needled into a tumor,
ticking?

Helical

What is the Covenant? I fain would learn.
That's the handshake deal we struck with God,
wherein we agreed to grovel in return
for being named His Favorite Tetrapod.

What are the Homeric Hymns? I ask.
These are a record of the consequence
when Middle School emotions wear the mask
of Heaven. Heaven knows how that tale ends.

The double-helix of the West!—two strands,
rooted in old pots, long intertwining,
rise like smoke from fire in the Holy Lands,
rise like spinal nerves whose braid, defining

what soul dipped in earth can know—*life*—
whose wick we may cut, once we have enough knife.

Necessity

Re: *rain*, and the long theological stalemate
concerning its origins, a tale Talmudic
in nuance, Homeric in scope: this was classic Lachrymism
vs. vulgar Micturism, paired like the chromosomes
of our tradition. At stake: the nature of Heaven.
At issue: the source of life, in rain. In the event,
the conclusive stroke was dealt by the geochemists,
who by the closing years of the last century had amassed
data demonstrating the identity of rain and tears
to the 97th part, in a theorem which survived rigorous peer
review. By contrast, undistilled urine assayed
as correlative only to the 60th part, notwithstanding acid
precipitates, adjusted mathematically, allowing for a salt-
correction constant. The question was settled.
Of course, rear-guard Micturian die-hards and tenured
professors with careers at stake and minds too inured
to the old way of thinking continued to cavil. Attempts
to impeach experimental procedure failed. Die or adapt:
the science proved solid. And we were happy, were we not?
Sure, though Heaven knows one cannot count on Nature
to conform to human preference, none could deny
a private relief at the proof: the tragic mind of Adonai
might henceforth be petitioned. The vulgar Eiron
was cast down. Earth bloomed. Heaven wept pure thereon.

*

The droughts began in the second decade following.
Crops failed in successive seasons. Fields lay fallow.
We attempted public supplications, under open skies,
the sadness of our plight sharpened by rhetors, our cries
drawn taut by singing masters, our kennings
pitched by poets to the asymptote of pity, razor-keen.
Still God withheld His tears. We sacrificed.
We burned incense, livestock, houses, towns. We revisited
more ancient screeds. With stricken reluctance
unimaginable to any human not so fated, we looked
into the red eye of Necessity, and agreed to begin
sacrificing the children again.

*

We will not be judged. Our lamentations exonerate us. Arraign
ineluctable fact in the court of the real. Physics
was never of our choosing. We must have rain
or die. One must live in the world as it is.

Questions for Delphi

1

Sing, Muse—

          If we, while thinking a thing untrue,

try it on the face of the world,

willing the lie may ameliorate that future

fissuring sheer before us, that black beckon,

begging only that our poppycock not seem too arrant,

our rants and ritual mutterings and queer ceremonial suits too risible—

Sibyl, speak: tell me, when we do that—

                      do we do right?

2

To repeat:

When drives dress themselves in a few abstractions,
bridle themselves with a few thready strictures

and get themselves promoted to the prefrontal cortex
salaried as *ideas*, diacritics

over serotonin, so to speak, sophist
shaking his shaman's rattle in the high glass office—suffice

it to say, we have *civilization*.
When such *ideas,* exhaled against the sky's silvering

precipitate in clouds. . . .
That is, when ideas graduate as gods,

garbed in the advanced fashions of the upwardly mobile,
braille-bright, labile

as one would expect of a personified whirl-
wind, as it were—

well, that circle would seem complete.

3

In a more up-to-date case:

When we make of a magma and mantle planet
a guise called *Gaia,*
when we propose of her gas-lit slime-thin skim of biology

a god to adore,
adorning our postures and censures with sanctimony
in Her name

do we vouchsafe a future for our children?
Chill
the answers

on the question's face.

Madonna in Blue

An aneurysm in the sun, a gravity-wave.
A beating of rainbows against the windowpane.
The angel, a lunge, an ejaculation of lilies, kneels,
knowing. Nods past her upstretched palm: he *knows*.

Against her will her womb suborned by a god,
incubating a future so far-fetched and odd
how could its knowledge from its power culled
but show? Her pose: a cobalt spring recoiled.

And what should a watching voyeur feel then? Rage?
The Ovidian horror? Again the seized girl, again Kore
covered by ungoverned god, as known is by strange,
as Past by Future—*this* one, where there are no angels,
no seraphim but us, its mobbing choir?
What *happened*? Didn't the painter's brush catch fire?

The Birth of Tragedy

Syntax rides mahout on an ancient python,
wrestling that sine-wave till it's kenned
a superscript, encoded in the writhing
muscle of emotional intent.

And so *Pan sapiens* invents *tomorrow*,
and *yesterday*, and *Rome*, and *maybe not*,
and all the grammars swaddling his sorrows
in that abyss between what is and ought.

But in the petri dish where glass pipettes
drop glucose *here*, and *here* a drop of lye,
the little one-celled creature senses death,
and edges toward a future otherwise.

The Greeks knew this, who copied faithfully
the diptych of the ancient primate mask:
one *Yes*, one *No*. Hath holy Pythia
another answer, ever? We can ask.

Meanwhile, in the Pantheon, a moment later
made its difference. As so it did to Rome.
As so, to moon: see now, *the terminator
cuts across her like a microtome.*

XI.

VANISHING

Another moon—sssh—

hear crescent, *then* crescent?*—that's*

the sound of the shears.

Follow-up Questions for the Pythia

Does money make greed possible—
the germ, itself, of the sin?
Or simply make greed visible,
as confetti would, wind?

Did syntax set the human mind,
with music, painting, dance?
Do verbs spin the cogs of time
or only track a trance?

What's fire? A magic hat?
Does *burn* mean *oxidize*?
What flickers in the ziggurat
of carbon, in the eyes?

Is love love without embrace?
Can love live in reserve?
May certain values be their face?
What's courage, lacking nerve?

I wish I knew. I'd bet good money
on dreams without a snoozing,
dreams like some folks, who, unfunny,
sometimes are amusing:

sometimes the world's hidden fees
are queasy in our sleep;
sometimes they say it won't be easy
when they mean it won't be cheap.

Meanwhile, I'll watch a bunch of birds
kerfuffle down a breeze
astir like metal in the purse
to vanish in some trees.

Good as a Mile

The sky replies to questions posed
by human senses, only those.
The sky is coy that way. It gulls.
It flimmers to the human pulse.

As nights are that which is not days,
the mirror dimples to our gaze.
Cast and casting; call, response,
candle daylit in the sky's sconce—

Askance I saw it, then. How else?
(the steering-wheel was carousels)—
our complement is all outdoors;
a fair likeness, too, of course.

Here's a story, by the bye
of how a mote caught in my eye—

*

Today, driving, I glimpsed the moon.
A half-moon, to be more precise,
small smear on an afternoon—

And all of a sudden as it struck my eyes
it wasn't *the moon,*
man-tracked, myth-worn, penny-sized,

nor retinal nick, nor rhyme on *rune,*
but a rock on the windshield, white as the Christ,
an immense, nonce, fully round

planetary thing,
locked in a gravitational partner-swing
with everything.

*

Not "the moon," I'm telling you! Not a pale communion-wafer,
but an astral entity, curving, stippled, dented, an entire rock
sky yawing steeply away on the shadowed side, adrift. It was
bigger than gibbous. It looked sensational as one of those
artist's impressions of "Callisto rising, as seen from the surface
of Ganymede." It felt like science fiction. I almost swerved
the car.

*

Can I hope to make you see this as I did?
Haven't you, too, yawned late, to witness—what,
some astral smirch or other—forecast aurora—
aphelion eclipse—the guaranteed closest approach
of Mars, or Jupiter, or any dirty comet
pinking its horizon, per advertisement,
commending mind to empyrean,
murmuring wan words like *there?*—then
there? forefingering night—well, haven't you?—
and, just as in this failed linguistic instance,
missed it?

What Am I?

On a blue glass beach
a prehistoric shark tooth
you can't reach?

The Candle in Daylight

Only look askance. Can't
see it otherwise. Crescent
on the wrought sky-sconce—

flakelike paring—moth-
wing—windscreen with wet petal—
glacial tablecloth's

crisp fabric cobwebbed
in what icewater-pitchers
aclink with ice cubes

do: *that* hyaline,
membranous skirting, unsquare
whirl, linen alive

with it, the flicker-
of likening, the not-there
of it, the for-lack-

of-words delighting,
blue future's egg-tooth, truth, the
candle in daylight.

Slow Blue

As time's canopy
where the cut tree shivering
slightly can appear

stopped: that blink eon
before stupendous motion,
so this saurian

slow blue, the heron,
when the breast muscle ignites
its deep furnace here,

and the tidepool soughs
and stirs, and the long eyelid
of the wing lifting.

Plants, Animals

Consider this:
if the fibrillating willow,
water as it mostly is,

is a sort of slow
fountain,
that leaves all of us, aloft, alow

—if, granted,
swifter over the ground,
moreover—

more of a river.

Other Water Clocks

Rings

Drips from a shipped oar
behind the gliding dory:
little orrery.

Prairie

Gone sea. Corn stubble.
The tidal rip's strong here still,
if resistible.

Hulk in Estuary; Horizon

What's disorganized
from wood boat to nails in mud?
Old wild surmise.

Moon and Stars

From Tree Full Moon

Luteal (if not
at all unlutely) lifting
from its little net.

*

Dryad Impossible

A starlit forest's
photosynthesis?—slight surge,
sugar to the root?

Tidal

Patient, the sea-seiche,
sorting according to size
cobbles down the beach.

Here's Ocean's wheeze—seas
clicking into sentient speech
in Demosthenes—

Think, then, tide on stone,
self-organizing no end.
Large; small; smaller; none.

And More Vivalding

1. Symphonic

March upcrumples expostulate sky
like a mongoose on a doily,
welcoming sun as thumb to eye,
while treating robins roily.

Green ferns bend a breeze
under summer's awning;
windows wide in libraries
and books and hammocks yawning.

Autumn whooms in fire first,
sumac, oak, and maple:
napalm bloom soon doused in mist,
and rain straight as cable.

Solstice doldrum, wool-chill,
the world in cold pajamas,
her icicles all prism-still
as air is, after hammers.

2. Redirect

What's the point of penning verse
like this? Why not erasures?
Something edgy, fresh, fierce,
on sex, or race, or glaciers?

If we'll just slice the spinal nerve
the sun'll settle still.
It won't bank, swoop, or swerve.
We'll study it at will.

That's good advice. Cerebral. Apt.
All rhyme I'll soon rescind-O . . .
I'd do it now, except I keep
glancing out the window.

The Graving Yard

FOR JOHN DELANEY

1. The Oceanographer

An ocean's pumped back in. Immense placental
engines labor. Lubbers, we have shore-leave until
midnight, when we'll board, too. Mantid cranes
wipe sky. One sways up the submersible,
belling. More cable-whine and whistle. Vessel groans
against its wharf.
                          Below, empty sample-
bottles chatter a little on a steel bench.
At 2°C in a berth below in the black benthos
of the napping oceanographer's dream, crimson
tubeworms, bacterial mansions, impossible basalt
spires outgassing. Archaeozoan something-or-others. Drumskin
lithospheres slipping on their puddings far from the Esquimault
Graving Yard, in a watery, igneous elsewhere, in a sherbet
of ammonia, maybe, on the second moon of Jupiter.

2. *Anaerobe*

You, yolk
too, sound
in the steel bubble
submersible.
Touch swollen tonsils:
gill slits.
Inside eyelid: slimelight.
Cheek: shark.
Here foreknown
we've dived
down dawnless
microbial snows,
phosphor blue to blue-
black, to black.
Fend fish. Find
the saffron curb
of the sulfur vent,
veering voiceless
again into the segmented,
swaying, white,
toothed tube-
worm, Time.

—*should die,* she laughs, *I shall go to heaven,*
which sounds not only confident, but gallant,
too, until you think about it, given
the difference in our ages. A land
of unlikeness. What would that be, for her? A blessed
realm, I suggest, turgid with ski instructors, solar
energy entrepreneurs, and software moguls
with mighty abs and intelligent eyes, their opalescent
intentions confessed in wines aswirl, from cellars
certified in France, n'est-ce pas? *My goal's*
otherwise, she says, growing serious,
which is the last thing either of us wants. Thin
smiles ensue. The land of unlikeness, eerie
as ever. But *really*? she says. Really? What, then?

Vanish, then? Live alone among strangers?—
tap an umbrella on the porches of old hotels,
the kind with tea-rooms and oaken bannisters
and baths down the hall, anywhere not Paris? Oslo,
maybe, Pittsburgh . . . Pittsburgh?—no, Tangiers . . .
Which would it be? *Hygge* by the purpling Jøtul,
watching fjord-fog crawl, or swirling anisette
in a sweating glass on a lime-white, blinding terrace, slow
ceiling fan batting at the noon stun?
                                              Tinctures
of the fountain pen, that water-clock: you'd tell
it longhand, in a blank book titled *Finisterre,*
that phantasy of anywhere not home, solo,
quotidian, fossicking that lifelong midden,
dabbing at doing what I said I'd do, and didn't?

Love

Bees thick enough to cast
a shredding shadow on the grass.

Migrating birds on Doppler radar.
The Little Bear above the Greater.

The full moon muzzy through the fog.
Droplets off a shaking dog.

The seconds off the clock's éclat . . .
Like anything particulate

these things have shapes, but they don't have edges.
So, what does? Give me a *such as:*

The razor, slicing, feels no skin.
The noun seems neither out nor in.
Where does anything begin?

Parting Glass

MAEVE

Here's to the leopard who'd launder his spots,
the proactive traveler packing some prunes;
here's to gazpacho in coppery pots,
here's to the helium bobbing balloons.

Here's to the moons of Jupiter, here's
to the whistling steeplejack waving his cap.
Skoal to starshine, sharp as shears,
and the heat on the hearthstone upholstered in cat.

Here's to the pollster who's wondering whether;
here's to the whiskery frost on the pane.
Here's to your shadow, and here's to its tether;
here's to the thuddery roof under rain.

Woof to your mother and thump to my sons,
and kisses for maidens, their aprons askew;
salutes to some strangers I may have met once,
and a glass for my ghosts and pookas—boo:

Toast to my tailor whose needle's bespoke,
for Adam and Eve and the coop that they flew;
clink to the mirror whose dubious joke
is leaving me less of a him than a who,

who hopes you'll perceive, Maeve, it's hardly adieu
(and this is the magic, all mirror and smoke)
when the glass is the goblet he's raising to you.

Vanishing Point

CAROL

The kissed fingerpad
touched wet with wine
orbiting a crystal rim: ring,
ring,
a shuddering wrung into rhyme,
a moment's longbow
drawn to vanishing.

Annus Mirabilis

In this place still called *The*
Pantheon,
where once upon

a time it was no pinhole *camera*
obscura clamorous
with French, American

and Japanese, we wed
with no priest but old words
and a witness. What

place was that? Not this,
exactly. Thus
is the analog light-stream digitized. *The*

(we said) *Pantheon,*
and kissed therein. Then
Time, the god-yawn.

Signs

The Perseids are cinders, now,
the summer stars dissolved in wine,
the conflagration of the bough
extinguished in an Autumn rain.

Orion's back in the black. Behind,
where moonshine suffocates in cloud,
sling other nouns, like Charles's Wain
(or Bear, as some prefer, or Plough).

Below—blind. What words occlude!
Stars tangle in the trees' runes,
rising, setting. . . . Our ups and downs
were never in their lights aligned.

Mind how the breeze outside bassoons
and susurrates this cozy house.
It swoons like a tuning fork whose tines
twist in wind, or a wand whose dowse

divines love, instead of water,
divines love, instead of future,
divines nothing in these signs.

Acknowledgments

I'm indebted to the S. Wilson and Grace M. Pollock
Endowment at the University of Washington for support
during the decade of this book's assembly. I'm especially
grateful to colleagues and friends at the Friday Harbor
Laboratories, whose hospitality has meant much to me, and to
the Helen Riaboff Whiteley Center there, where many of these
poems were written or chastened. For those rigors, salutes to
Carol Light, Jason Whitmarsh, and Cody Walker, to whom the
book owes much of its shape. For the rest, a grateful wave to
Deb Garrison, Todd Portnowitz, Bonnie Thompson, and Rita
Madrigal at Knopf.

Warm thanks to Mott Greene (my Geometer, in "The Drake
Equation") and Adam Summers, for long and patient science
advisory. Also to Sholeh Wolpe, who walked me through the
literal translation of the Rumi poem, and to Christopher
Merrill at the International Writing Program, whose auspices
in partnership with the U.S. State Department made that
occasion possible.

The scraps stitched into the cento on pages 132 and 133
originate in Larkin, Auden, and Frost.

Finally, I'll thank the editors of the following magazines,
where many of the poems were accepted for first publication,
some in earlier versions or under different titles:

Agni: "Muted," "Leadership," "Another Sunset"

The Antioch Review: "Cave, Reversed" originally published as "Chiaroscuro," "*Pan sapiens* 2," "Questions for Delphi," "Follow-Up Questions for Pythia"

The Hampden-Sydney Poetry Review: "Cubicle," "Blackboard," "Farm," "D-Train," "Gym," and "Surgery" originally published together as "Places." A selection of chapter-section epigraphic verses, "Our Shimmer of Days," "From Sound Sleep, Isaac," "Sales Spike with the Toll," "Another Soon: Sssh," "Hobbes Obtrudes. Rousseau," and "There's Nothing Any," originally published together as "Six Discouraging Epigrams."

The Hopkins Review: "The Bad News, Straight," "Science Tuesday"

Light: "Boy Toys," "Tattered Coat"

Mare Nostrum: "The," "From Tree Full Moon," "Rings"

The Monarch Review: "Poetaster in Paris," "The Arcturan Vivesectionist Explains," "Global Citizen," "It's Always Yourself That You Find in the Sea," "Foreboding"

Narrative: "Easter Wings," "How?" "Vanishing Point," "The Apparition of These Faces," "Spring Wedding," "When I Lose," "Jeopardy," "Family Men," "Money, Worse," "Time Change," and "Vanishing Point." "December's Plans" and "May's Plans" originally published together as "Plans."

The New Criterion: "Numbers"

Plume: "If One of Us," "Madonna in Blue," "A Winter's Tale" and epigraph for Section VII first appeared as "And That?" as part of "Six Blessings"

Poetry: "The Drake Equation," "Anaerobe," "March"

Poetry Northwest: "Plants, Animals," "Day Moon," "Other Water Clocks" originally published as "Waters," "Slow Blue," "And More Vivalding," "Very Well, Thank You," "Memento Mori," "Love," "Afterlife," "Sword Upstairs"

The Sewanee Review: "Necessity"

Slate: "I'm Going to Have to Fire the Dream Master"

Southwest Review: "Annunciation"

Terrain: "Definitions," "Good as a Mile," "Terminator," "Tidal"

The Yale Review: "Pax," "Afterlife," "Over Coffee"

Author's Note

Outtake, Concerning This Book's Aggressive Title:

Hat-swoops to Hollywood!—that's de rigueur,
I guess. Regards to Mr. Schwarzenegger,

by all means, no *mens sana* meatier.
My title, though (see Wikipedia)

refers to the other firmament, where a moon's
chiaroscuros curve like nesting spoons—

I'll illustrate. Pretend it's night. Look up,
like the man-moth, eyeball pressed against the egg-cup

moon. Now gently drape your optic nerve
across that vocative, like so: not curved

across the middle, like the letter θ
(that's, as any kid knows, the *equator*),

but rather pole-to-pole, like uppercase Φ:
That line's **the terminator**. It defines

a moving shadow, shearing light from dark,
the day/night line. You'll note its crawling arc

(which sickles everything) bisects this book,
too—the valley down the middle, if you look.

*

That valley splits the mirror halves of the poem titled
"Memento Mori." Here I tried to do in words what I saw in
Florence once, in paint. I've never found that panel again; I'll
imagine it tucked away in the Uffizi's Renaissance attic. Like
a number of other trompe l'oeil works of the period (not to
mention winking refrigerator art of the 1950s), the painting
was figured on a corrugated surface, which made the two-for-
one trick possible: standing to one side, you'd see a lovely young
woman; moving across, you'd see her turn to bones. Passersby
often did a double take, sidling back to find that point in the
arc where both apparitions vanish.

At any rate, this book attempts something like the same trick.
It's divided into chapters, five on either side of the medial abyss.
This is partly to keep sugars from vinegars, and partly to check
exhaustion—following Poe, it seemed to me that a long book
might hospitably be measured in a string of "single sittings,"
one coffee spoon each, and that's my recommendation here.

Last caveat: When Freud amusedly writes to his wife, "If one
of us should die, I shall go to Paris," it's one thing. When in
Frost's "Home Burial," the speaker to his wife predicts, "I shall
laugh the worst laugh I ever laughed," it's another. Death and
its modal auxiliary have lighter and darker shades, and so have
these poems. If *chiaroscuro* is the painter's word for it, those
syllables are in the correct order here: intermittent sunshine to
the left of the terminator; steady discouragement to the right,
remitting somewhat before moonset.

A NOTE ABOUT THE AUTHOR

Richard Kenney is the author of four previous books of poetry: *The Evolution of the Flightless Bird, Orrery, The Invention of the Zero,* and *The One-Strand River.* His work has attracted recognitions, among them the Yale Series of Younger Poets Prize, a Lannan Literary Award, the Rome Prize in Literature, and fellowships from the Guggenheim and MacArthur Foundations. He teaches at the University of Washington and lives with his family on the Olympic Peninsula.

A NOTE ON THE TYPE

The text in this book was set in Miller, a transitional-style typeface designed by Matthew Carter (b. 1937) with assistance from Tobias Frere-Jones and Cyrus Highsmith of the Font Bureau. Modeled on the roman family of fonts popularized by Scottish type foundries in the nineteenth century, Miller is named for William Miller, founder of the Miller & Richard foundry of Edinburgh.

Composed by North Market Street Graphics,
Lancaster, Pennsylvania

Printed and bound by Berryville Graphics,
Berryville, Virginia

Book design by Pei Loi Koay